GW00455110

Disclaimer: This book has been written to help to explain the difficulties .... using "old" labels when describing dog behaviour. Every effort has been made to ensure its accuracy. Whilst the information in this book is, to the authors' knowledge, accurate at the time of writing, information changes and new facts arise which may supersede some of this book's content. Readers acting on any information contained within this book do so at their own risk. Your veterinarian should be consulted for advice. Neither the authors, nor the publisher, nor anyone providing recommendations for this book accepts any liability or responsibility to any pet, person or entity with respect to damage, loss, or injury caused or implied, or said to be caused directly or indirectly following the information contained here.

Illustrations: *Mandy Daveridge*

Editors:

Jackie Bennett DipCABT, Pet Behaviourist & Trainer, www.bellabehaviour.co.uk

Lorna Winter GLCM, LLCM, DipCABT

First edition published December 2017. Ardgay, Scotland.
Second edition published September 2018, Ardgay, Scotland.
(2 new chapters on Guilty & Punishment.)
ISBN-13: 978-1720808947 (Print Version)

www.facebook.com/DogzThinkzDifferentz

www.PawsAbility.co.uk/DogzThinkzDifferentz

Contents

About the Authors

Anna Patfield is a dog behaviourist, trainer and author. She developed a serious interest in dog behaviour around 2000, when she acquired a dog with behavioural problems. Moving on to study with COAPE (The Centre of Applied Pet Ethology), her passion for unraveling the mysteries broadened to incorporate the study of nutrition and its impact on behaviour. She has been helping dog and puppy owners since 2003 and authored "The Good Dog Diet", which clearly explains canine nutritional science and sorts out the facts from the myths.

Anna holds Advanced Diplomas in Companion Animal Behaviour & Training and Canine Nutritional Science with COAPE and CASI (The Companion Animal Sciences Institute), and is a full member of CAPBT (The COAPE Association of Applied Pet Behaviourists & Trainers).

www.PawsAbility.co.uk and www.TheGoodDogDiet.com

Helen Hitchings combines her love of teaching and animal behaviour by offering one-to-one behaviour therapy for cats and dogs and running lectures and workshops on pet themes.

She started her animal career in 1991 as a student vet nurse with PDSA, becoming a fully qualified Registered Veterinary Nurse (RVN) in 1994. Her journey into dog behaviour and training started in 1997 with Connor. Connor had had difficulties with his gun dog training and had lived in multiple homes before Helen found him. Working with Connor taught Helen that positive reinforcement and force-free training was the only way to go.

This led to studying with COAPE, qualifying in 2002 with a Diploma in Companion Animal Behaviour and Training (DipCABT), refreshing this qualification in 2015. Helen has also taught Behaviour & Nursing units on the Animal Management Diploma course, gaining qualified teacher status (Cert Ed) at Portsmouth University in 2008, and became a Certified Trainer with Victoria Stilwell Positively Dog Training in 2016, where she is now a mentor.

www.PetBehaviourServices.com

Natasja Lewis's interest in dog training started around 23 years ago with her Shetland Sheepdog Dali, who led the way into a life of dog training and behaviour. She breeds and shows Groenendaels, winning Best of Breed at Crufts in 2009 and 2010. She has also competed in obedience, rally obedience and agility, and became a Dog Show Judge in 2015.

Natasja gained her Advanced Diploma in Companion Animal Behaviour and Training through COAPE in 2009 and has been a member of CAPBT ever since. She is passionate about making training fun for dogs and owners, and now uses concept and games based training in all her classes. Natasja specialises in puppy training, has a keen interest in dog behaviour, and is always seeking to further and update her knowledge by attending seminars and workshops in related topics.

www.nightsabre.co.uk

Mandy Daveridge is passionate about teaching and believes that understanding emotionality and clear communication in animals are vital in shaping behaviours.

She holds Bachelor degrees in modern languages and law (BA, LLB) and a Master's Degree in Business Administration (MBA). She recently successfully completed the COAPE Higher Diploma in Applied Clinical Pharmacology, Neurophysiology and Therapeutics in Companion Animal Behaviour Therapy (DipCABT (RQF Level 6)). She is a fully qualified Personal Trainer/Fitness Instructor with some 20 years experience in the Fitness Industry. She is also a certified Neuro Linguistic Programming (NLP) Practitioner.

She has lived with dogs all her life, and currently divides her time between working as a Dog Behaviourist/Trainer and a Personal Trainer.

www.maddogz.co.uk

Introduction

It's interesting, although perhaps not surprising, that the perception of how dogs think differs between pet owners and those trainers and behaviourists who have been studying and learning about canine brains and behaviour over the past 20 years or so. Knowledge has advanced, but the general public perception remains largely the same.

We all come across this every day. Pet owners apologise for letting their dogs up on the sofa, saying that they know they shouldn't because it makes their dogs *dominant*. Dogs are described as *stubborn* when they refuse to walk to heel, and people look for dog training classes to help *socialise* their aggressive dogs.

Now, perhaps there is some validity with these old terms, but what we tend to find is that these labels inhibit our ability to truly see what's going on. By taking a step back and looking for the real root cause of a behaviour, we can take a fresh approach. We can enhance what we are doing and perhaps achieve our goals more effectively.

This book aims to help fill that gap in perception in the following areas, so that:

1. Pet owners seeking help for their dogs may begin to learn that the knowledge of dog behaviour and training has changed. Also for those who choose to use labels like *dominance* and *stubborn*, to consider different ways of thinking so they can start to see inside their dog's mind more clearly.

2. Pet professionals, including some dog behaviourists, trainers and others working with dogs, may begin to consider the difficulties with these old-school labels. We hope the discussion and practical examples within this book will provide new perspectives regarding how to tackle the problems. For those who already work this way, we hope that this book will be a useful reference for you to pass on to others.

3. We may help to calm the debate about the words we use. Even modern "positive" trainers and behaviourists spend time arguing over labels. Let's move forward, rebrand these terms, and focus more on solutions.

Of course this book will only begin to convey the issues with these controversial terms. We will outline the issues, discuss the problems with the terminology and suggest some simple solutions. It is not the aim of this book to provide detailed behaviour or training programmes for *timid* or *stubborn* dogs, nor to discuss *socialisation* or the use of *rewards* in detail.

It's simply meant to be a lighthearted summary, to give us food for thought and to sow some new ideas. There are, after all, many different potential solutions. So if you are having problems, please do seek out a qualified and experienced behaviourist or trainer to help.

So please read on to gain a better insight into dogs' brains and hopefully begin to comprehend how this new knowledge will help us to resolve our doggy difficulties. In addition, please do share this book widely to help us to spread the word and de-bunk those old school dog training and behaviour myths. Hope you enjoy ☺

He's Dominant

We think: *My dog always jumps on me and pulls me along.*

Dogz Think: *Heyz, I just wanna have cuddles like we used to when I woz a puppy & I wanna get to the park fast to play with my pals.*

What are we talking about?

It seems that many, many pet dog owners "know" that when dogs present certain behaviour problems that they are being *dominant*. Any time that a dog pulls or jumps or refuses to come back to them or get off the sofa, they think their dog is trying to get one over them or be the leader of the pack.

What's really going on?

This is a real conundrum in the dog behaviour and training world. Yet, it actually seems that dominance and punishment-based dog training methods only became part of the dog-training world at the beginning of the 20th century. Even at that time there was significant disagreement with regard to dogs and emotion. However, these dominance methods were promoted very effectively via successful book marketing and later, TV programmes. Then, about 90 years later, prominent behaviourists and trainers came to realise that a) dogs are affected emotionally by the world around them and that b) they learn most effectively when they are rewarded for desirable behaviours.

Those of us working in this business and following this ethos see successful outcomes time and time again, but getting this message across to the public at large seems almost impossible. Sadly some courses on dog behaviour continue to teach pack leader theory, and the old methods are still picked up by some TV producers. Old books are republished as new and there is a constant drip-feed of the old theories. Perhaps we all resist change? Perhaps we see a wolf in our living room and gel with the old ideas of wolf pack hierarchy? (Which is actually wrong, but that's another story.) Yet it seems astonishing really that TV shows and a couple of books have had such a profound effect on the way we treat dogs.

Of course there are a few dogs that seem to have the desire or need to control things around them. For instance: guarding toys or food; looking for trouble on walks; or barking and lunging at owners when they leave the house. However, the reasons for these behaviours are most often better explained by boredom, fear, frustration, anger and so on, than by wanting to *dominate*.

What's the problem?

First, using the word *dominant* seems to make us feel that we need to deal with the issue using force. We feel that *we* need to dominate the situation. Yet, why do we need to think like that? Why should we want to *dominate* our dogs instead of living in peace and harmony? Many pet owners think this way even though they fundamentally know that their dogs can be happy or sad.

Second, some feel that there are generic rules that can be applied to *fix* dominant dogs. These consist of exercises such as eating before the dog, never letting him walk in front of you, and never letting him out the door first. Whilst the latter provides some measure of safety, none of these exercises addresses how the dog is actually feeling.

Further, it prevents us from analysing individual situations, each of which may well have a different cause. A dog may be angry, thinking that his food may be stolen, but excited when going to the park. Changing these behaviours requires different approaches, depending on the underlying emotion.

So, what can we do about our dominant dogs?

Well, we need to change our mindsets. We need to consider the emotional motivation behind the behaviour. We need to change our dogs' environments to help them to start to think differently; to help them to feel more calm and relaxed; to not be anxious; to not be bored or frustrated.

Possessive aggressive dogs are frequently bored. Dogs who behave aggressively towards people or dogs are frequently scared. Dogs who are aggressive on lead are frequently frustrated.

By taking these feelings on board we can start to change how we think about them. We can change what we do to help them feel differently and no longer feel the need to behave in this undesirable way. Here are some examples:

Jumping up on you

Dogs jump up either to get to our faces or to get more body contact and because jumping on other dogs is a common way to play. But, fundamentally, we teach them this behaviour when they are puppies. We pick them up and cuddle them and help them to learn that having their body on ours is really nice. That's it. Nothing more. We can easily prevent this issue arising when they are puppies by simply keeping their four paws on the floor and giving our cuddles there. When they are older it can help to teach them that all they need to do to get our attention is to put their bottom on the ground. Admittedly, that can be difficult and may require a wee training lesson or two!

A dog on the bed

Simply put, our bed is a comfy, cosy place where the dog can feel happily enveloped in our scent. There's nothing wrong with a dog being on our bed (if we're happy with that) unless they have some behavioural problem such as aggression or separation issues. In which case, there may be complications that require professional help.

Walking in front, pulling us along

Just consider how a dog feels when they go out for a walk. Some dogs can become very excited when going to the park, the hills or saying hello to the dog at the end of the road. They are just much more motivated than us to walk and sniff and get to play in the park. But, despite the many successful reward-based methods that have been used to teach a nice heel position, many pet owners seem to persist with a stop-and-jerk approach. Just think about that. Why would a dog want to walk beside us when they've just had their neck jerked? Surely it's far better to teach them that being beside our leg is really great?

A dog is guarding food

Here we need to teach them that it's good to have us around their food bowl. Taking it away from them simply serves to fuel the anger. Please do take care here. Intense anger needs a cautious approach and may well benefit from professional advice.

He Hates the Postie or Cats or the Vacuum

We think: *My dog hates these things so much because he is barking, growling, lunging at, or chasing them.*

Dogz Thinkz: Postie: *There must be something very wrong wiv thiz guy. He never comez in - he must not be a friend - I better get rid of him! Cats: Yeah, a catz, I lurv to chase them catz! Vacuum: Geez, that noise is scary!*

What are we talking about?

Postie: Some dogs bark or growl when the postie comes to the door or passes by or perhaps they grab and shred the mail.

Cats: Dogs may strain on a lead or try to chase a cat.

Vacuum: He growls and lunges at the vacuum.

What's really going on?

Postie: The postie comes along, the dog barks, the postie leaves. Our dogs come to believe that it's their barking that ensures that this scary person goes away. We may even help them to believe this way because we run to the door (to save the post), or shout (albeit at the dog to be quiet). Or, indeed, it may simply be a bit of fun in an otherwise boring day!

Cats: Dogs instinctively love to chase small furry things that move. They're not really thinking about what they're doing other than perhaps thinking "food"! It is quite possible, therefore, that a dog chasing a cat is just enjoying the thrill of the chase. (Of course, we consider that to be unacceptable.)

Vacuum: Many dogs are scared of noises such as fireworks, thunder, cooker pings, telephones, ironing boards or our very noisy vacuums. So they bark or lunge at the vacuum and guess what? It works! At some point, we switch it off, put it away, and the noise stops. Of course, we may also encourage our puppies to chase it because we think it's funny (at the start).

What's the problem?

Well, you may have realised by now that this little book is about considering the difficulty with labels. It tends to stop us thinking about the nuances of what might actually be going on and reduces the options we may have when trying to change an unwanted behaviour.

After all, the word *hate* may convey so many different thoughts. We may *hate* a person, we may *hate* spiders, we may *hate* potholes, we may *hate* the thought of going to the gym, or we may *hate* nuisance phone calls. There are so many different contexts.

It's not surprising, therefore, that we use this generic word to describe different scenarios in our dogs' lives. Do we, perhaps use the word *hate* when we feel helpless about a particular situation? There's nothing we can do to get the potholes fixed or those unwanted nuisance phone calls to stop!

Hate and anger are not, it seems, as well understood as fear. There is discussion regarding whether animals have the capacity to *hate* and how complex that feeling may be, yet it is unlikely that dogs have the human capacity to scheme and plan.

For our purposes then, we may benefit from simply ditching the label. We can then open our thoughts and analyse how the dog *feels* in a particular situation. Dogs may indeed decide to persistently attack another dog in the house, but most often there are several factors involved other than just pure *hate*.

So, how can we help our dogs that seem to hate certain things?

First, we need to understand the actual root of the problem. Asking these questions provides so many more potential solutions. We can work on boredom or fear or toy competition. We can also help them to learn what we actually want them "to do" instead of just shouting at them or saying "No! Stop it!" all the time. Here are some ideas for what to do with the most common targets:

The Postie

1. Keep the dog well away from the letterbox area until the postie has been.

2. Work on helping the dog to ignore the noise of the letterbox.

3. Teach the dog to go and lie down and stay on his bed. Gradually build on the training so that he can do that when the letterbox rattles.

At the end, we can all relax when the postie comes.

The Cat

1. Consider where this is happening. If it's when walking along the street, start off by going for walks elsewhere. This will help calm the initial problem and prevent habits continuing. Then follow step 2.

If it's in the garden, then make sure you get out first and move the cat away.

2. Work on general heel and recall training. Build on this step by step, introducing various distractions to build self-control. Once your dog has more focus on you, then start to work on various "stop-cat-chasing" exercises. Generally, this starts a good distance away, moving gradually closer (safely on lead of course). This can be a difficult goal to achieve and may need the help of a good trainer.

The Vacuum

1. Keep the dog out of the way when you need to vacuum.

2. Teach the dog to be happy lying in a comfortable place out of the way.

3. Help the dog to feel calm with the vacuum by introducing it very quietly whilst keeping him occupied with something nice like a tasty chew. Then increase the noise and movement in very small steps.

Of course, these examples are highly simplified and the prognosis depends on the depth of the feeling and the length of time the behaviour has been practised. The more difficult situations will benefit from the help of a good behaviourist or trainer.

On a final note though, there is one scenario where the word *hate* may be a completely valid label: resolving aggression between two female dogs living in the same house, when there is no particular trigger. For whatever reason, this is probably the most difficult behaviour situation to resolve. Rehoming one of them is frequently the best overall solution.

He's Just Play Biting

We think: *It hurts a bit but it's ok or he's constantly biting me - he is a monster!*

Dogz Think: *But this iz how I play with my dog palz.*

What are we talking about?

Many dog owners see play biting as a vicious and aggressive behavior. Some think it's fine. Others don't realise that they are teaching their puppy it's ok to play-bite by playing rough and tumble games. Sometimes we expect an older dog to teach a puppy not to bite his ears; sometimes that works, sometimes it doesn't.

What's really going on?

Biting and mouthing are a natural part of puppy behaviour; helping him to learn about the world he lives in. A puppy uses his mouth to investigate and explore the world around him. It's a very exciting place for him, learning as he explores the environment and the things he finds in it. When he finds something new, you can almost hear him thinking as he tries to figure this new exciting thing out: "Hmm... what is this? Can I eat it?" (chomp chomp chomp). "No? Maybe I can play with it?" (Shakes it around whilst holding in mouth). "Can I make it run?" (Puppy pounces on our trouser legs or shoe laces.)

Playing with you and play fighting with other puppies will help your dog to develop coordination, reflexes and physical skills, allowing him to learn about acceptable and unacceptable behaviour. Sometimes the play biting and mouthing behaviours directed towards us can be quite scary and we might be forgiven to think that our puppy has turned into a manic fiend! Indeed, sometimes it does get out of hand. It's just like a group of kids playing, where you can see things getting out of control as their excitement grows.

What's the problem?

Many times we inadvertently teach puppies to bite and nip us when they are playing. We frequently play with them with our hands and feet – even when we don't mean to. (A puppy grabs at a sleeve and we almost play tug with them). So, these excited puppies get our attention when they pull on our clothes, hair and even grabbing our skin; it's rewarding for them.

So, sometimes puppies do not learn that play biting with humans is not socially acceptable. They continue to bite and mouth into adulthood, potentially leading to behavioural problems or at least, use their mouths in unacceptable circumstances. Puppies do not only need to learn to control the force of their biting but also that biting and mouthing people is not good, and frequently not acceptable with other dogs. This control is something we call "bite inhibition" and it is a very important skill for puppies to learn.

So, what can we do about our play biting and mouthy puppies?

There are some different circumstances to consider.

Puppy and dog interaction. We usually expect and hope that Mum, the littermates and other dogs will let a puppy know when they are being too rough in their play or get too excited and bite too hard. The bitten puppy squeals, the game stops for a few seconds and the puppy learns not to bite so hard next time. Or when the puppy is playing with a dog and nipping at their ears, we hope that the older dog will give a very mild growl and the puppy will listen. However, both these interactions require that the puppy is actually able to realise what these lessons mean. Frequently that doesn't happen. Here, we need to step in and prevent the games getting out of hand. We need to manage the puppy's excitement level and keep the play calm enough or step in and stop the game.

Puppy and human interaction. Your puppy needs to learn that biting really hurts! Every time your puppy bites your hand or mouths at your clothing we need to let them know that it hurts. Many times we can mimic a puppy response: when he bites at us we can "squeal" or "yelp", turn away to nurse our wounds and then ignore him for a few seconds. You will find that after a few of these lessons your puppy will stop mouthing you as soon as you say "ouch", they might even offer you a little lick instead of a bite. When this happens reward your puppy for stopping the biting and mouthing and continue to interact with them. However, this mimic-a-puppy method sadly doesn't always work. Some puppies get too much of a fright and some get more frustrated and continue to bite. For these puppies, management and careful play-training is a better approach.

Playing with your puppy will give you another brilliant opportunity to teach them about not biting you. The trick here is to play with a large (appropriate) toy and to teach him that he is allowed to mouth the toy that you are playing with but that your hands, clothes and arms are out of bounds. As your puppy learns this lesson he will no longer accidentally catch your hands as they move around playing with him and the toy. In fact your puppy will learn that playing with you and his toy is much more fun. This play really helps to develop your bond with your puppy.

This biting and mouthing behaviour will not disappear overnight. Rather, over the next 3 to 4 weeks he should gradually reduce the intensity of the bite as he starts to realise that putting teeth on you is not allowed.

If you have followed the above advice and you are still experiencing problems or your puppy has already learned to bite to get attention, you will need a different approach.

For these pups we need to take the fun out of the behavior, so no laughing, squealing or shouting if your pup bites. As soon as he puts his mouth on you, even in play, all interaction must stop immediately. Completely ignore him. If he is persistent, walk away closing the door behind you as you leave the room (if that's safe of course). One of the things your puppy desires the most is your company so taking that away for a little while, will teach him that his choices have consequences; his choice to bite you (even in play) results in all interaction and attention stopping.

Be consistent! It will take many repetitions before your puppy understands that biting results in the loss of all the fun. But, please don't persevere with this on your own for too long before seeking help. Some puppies do become quite aggressive and others seem to find it hard to learn this lesson. The earlier this is tackled, the easier it will be to stop.

About Rewards

We think: *I don't want to bribe my dog or make them fat, they should just do as I ask because they love me. Plus - I don't want to carry food with me all the time.*

Dogz Think: *Hey, I lovez you okay, but why should I do what you want when therez so many interezting thingz out there?*

What are we talking about?

Many people are reluctant to use treats to *reward* or bribe their dog for doing something. They think that the dog should just understand them and do what they want, or do it because they love them. Many have used treat training a little, but find the dog is no longer interested as soon as they leave the comfort of their home.

What's really going on?

Traditional dog training methods did not use treats but instead relied on a pat on the head for good behaviour and (hopefully mild) punishment (for example, a tap on the nose or saying "Bad Dog") for doing the wrong thing. People are worried that if they start using treats, their dog will only do as he's told for food rewards. Indeed, many have seen that to be the case. Food rewards work indoors but not outside.

What's the problem?

I'll tell you a little secret. You go to work. You do this to earn a living and to be able to provide for your family and hopefully enjoy some of the nicer things in life. And, you get paid for doing this. This is your *reward*. Would you work all these hours for nothing? So, why would your dog do something for nothing?

Put simply, dogs do whatever behaviour they think will make them feel better such as a fun game or a tasty treat.

For example: A lovely cake has just come out of the oven and has been left on the worktop to rest. The dog smells that, jumps up, reaches and finds that with a little effort he can drag it onto the floor and eat it all up. From this one incident the dog learns that kitchen counters are a really good place to find food. It's something that will definitely be worth a regular check.

So, using treats in dog training helps them to realise that there is benefit in doing what we ask them.

The problem that we tend to come across is that we just can't provide the same *reward* as that stolen cake, or a rabbit in a field, or a group of playful dogs. Nor can we get our dog to take a treat when they are perhaps scared of some noise or traffic. These situations are just way too distracting.

So, what can we do about our distracted dogs?

For those of us who have already embraced a more positive approach, but are still worried about using treats, or find that they don't work sometimes, the answer is just around the corner.

Modern dog training techniques have come about from scientific research about how dogs learn. We now know that dogs will repeat a specific behaviour if they perceive it as rewarding; if it makes them *feel* better. Simply put "Behaviours that get rewarded, get repeated".

However, the r*eward* needs to be *rewarding* to the *dog*: the things that we as humans view as rewarding may not actually be that special to our dogs. The rewards that we use should really get our dogs excited. We want our dogs to be bright-eyed, ears pricked and tail wagging happily.

Rewards can be anything your dog desires, whether that is positive attention from you or an ultra-tasty cube of cheese or ham or a game of fetch or tug or anything in between!

There are a couple of aspects, though, that we frequently don't think about:

1. Reward values vary depending on the other distractions around at the time.
2. Dogs need training practice in many different places. A kitchen or garden recall is different from the beach or the field.

So, whilst using verbal praise or bits of his usual food might work at home, when we go out and about, we need to increase the value of the reward. Kibble in the kitchen but cheese on the beach; a kind word in the living room but a game of tug in the park.

The trick that allows us to succeed with our training, is to plan out a programme so that we can control the level of distraction. We start off at a very low level, and then gradually increase it over time, making sure that we don't overwhelm our dogs.

Therefore, we need to:

1. Figure out which reward our dog really desires.
2. Determine how that relates to the particular environment.
3. Keep the distraction level low enough so that he'll still work for the reward in that environment.
4. And then move on to helping him to learn in a wide variety of situations.

It's also crucial to remember when using treat-based training that we don't fall into the trap of continually luring our dogs with a piece of food in our hands. There is nothing wrong with luring a puppy's head up when holding a piece of food to encourage him to sit. But after the first few times, do away with the treat in your hand and only give it to him once he has offered you the sit. This way your puppy will learn what you are asking him to do, without having to rely on you having food in your hand at all times.

So what do we do when this doesn't work? Sometimes, a dog is simply overwhelmed or overexcited by all the sounds, sights and smells he is encountering. Other times, he may be anxious or worried. If the dog is overexcited we need to assess the environment for distractions and find a way to provide calmer surroundings so that he is still able to respond to us and accept rewards for good behaviour. If the dog is anxious then we need to take a step back, help them to overcome those fears and build up their confidence gradually.

About Socialisation

We think: My puppy or dog needs to play with lots of others so they learn to be tolerant of all dogs.

Dogz think: Hey, I lovez playing with other puppiez, I get so excited! Or weeelll, I like to take my time meeting others n hang back til I'm sure we'll get along. Those big dogz look scary.

What are we talking about?

Everyone knows that socialisation is an important part of puppy education. Many people think that this is just about letting our puppy have play dates with a few puppies and dogs. Some people, with several dogs at home, believe that this provides enough dog interaction. People with unfriendly or highly excitable dogs often think that taking them to a class and forcing them to meet other dogs will help to *socialise* them.

What's really going on?

Well, first, socialisation is much more than just dog and puppy interactions.

And second, puppy introductions can so often go wrong and may have a significant impact on how a dog copes with life. Unlimited, unsupervised and uncontrolled interactions between dogs can quickly turn a shy puppy into a scared puppy. It can also teach bold, confident and forward puppies to bully others. Also, some older dogs just won't be able to cope straightaway with being in closer proximity to other dogs.

What's the problem?

We often have very high expectations of how our puppies should behave around people and other dogs and household pets. We want them to be able to deal with whatever life throws at them and to be happy about it.

Yet, sadly, we often unwittingly force our dogs to deal with situations that they are quite frankly, not ready to face. We think we have to make them confront the object of their fear. We expect all older dogs to put an excitable puppy in its place. These experiences may simply be too much for our puppies or dogs and may adversely affect their behaviour in similar future situations and in general.

Furthermore, we tend to take the world around us for granted and don't consider that washing machines, vacuums, bin lorries or horses could be scary things.

So how can we effectively socialise our puppies?

The general use of the term *socialisation* actually deals with two distinct but equally important areas. First, puppies need to be sociable with the people and animals with whom they live, and second, they need to learn to get used to (and essentially ignore), lots of smells, sights and sounds that will form part of their lives. That one word refers to a significant range of experiences, many of which are frequently overlooked.

We used to consider the critical socialisation period to be 8-12 weeks but now know that teaching puppies about life experience should begin much earlier. This early period of life is associated with both rapid brain growth and the development of fear. After about 16 weeks, puppies are far more likely to be scared of things that they haven't yet encountered. Some individuals and some breeds (such as German Shepherds) develop fear at a much younger age.

It may help to think of there being four *socialisation* phases:

1. When the puppy is with the breeder. Choose a breeder who knows about and has a safe *socialisation* plan for the puppies.

2. When we first get our puppy home, before he is fully vaccinated. At this stage we need to take precautions to protect our new puppy from disease, so please do ask your vet about local risks before proceeding. Then consider ways of keep your puppy safe whilst also exposing him to life. For instance, we can start off by carrying him to different places, visiting safe friends' houses, having friends visit him, sitting with him in the back of the car, working through various household noises, and even using the various freely available puppy socialisation CDs and downloads.

3. Vaccinations are complete. When it's safe to go out and about, we need to work out a plan for our puppy, taking into account his individual personality.

4. General Life. This life exposure needs to continue at regular intervals throughout our dog's life so that they remain able to cope with lots of different life situations.

Our puppies learn these crucial *socialisation* skills from careful exposure to traffic, noisy places, new people, other animals and so on. What's needed may vary depending on where we live. In the countryside exposure to farm machinery, livestock, horse riders and walking on the road will be most important for a puppy. For city living, more emphasis should be placed on "city type" experiences, such as heavy traffic, crowds of people, trains and buses and sirens from emergency vehicles. However, every puppy should learn to cope with all these situations, as we never know when life might change. And - it can't be stressed enough – all of this needs to be carried out safely and gently, without ever forcing a puppy to "face his fears".

In fact, fearful, timid or shy puppies need careful handling. Some puppies are more susceptible to fears than others. Forcing them to face scary situations is counter-productive and will most likely increase their fear. Start off at a safe distance and let them tell you when they are ready to take a closer look, or distract them with play or training. Fussing and worrying over them can give them the wrong impression. Giving them plenty of positive experiences and avoiding negative experiences is the key to successful socialisation.

At the other end of the scale, we also need to take care that bold, confident puppies learn to be polite and not to run at people and dogs and jump all over them.

Fortunately, much of this has already been worked out for us. Have a look at www.thepuppyplan.com, or browse online for free puppy socialisation checklists.

So how can we effectively socialise our older/rescue dogs?

Many rescue dogs settle in to their new lives very well, but some have already developed habits and fears or, indeed, are rehomed from completely different environments. Some of these dogs may be able to cope with going to dog classes, but many others will find that environment just too much to cope with, and may become distracted, jumpy, barky or even aggressive. Overall, it's better to address the dog's fears first, before enrolling in class. A scared or angry dog can't think clearly, won't be able to process information or retain knowledge and the exposure may cause more fear.

Instead, a careful, gentle plan is needed to help them to gradually build their calm confidence.

He's Stubborn

We think: My dog knows what to do, he just won't do what I want.

Dogz Think: But it'z a rabbitzzzz!

What are we talking about?

Many folks say that their dog is *stubborn*, and what's wrong with that? For them it precisely describes the behaviour in question - where their dog is determined to continue on the present course, despite what they, the owners, may want! For instance:

- A dog standing looking between the owner and whatever is catching their attention (other dogs, a deer, a rabbit, a ball) and refusing to come back

- A dog manically digging at a carpet to get through a door to get to a ball

- Refusing to walk properly on the lead

However, there is a further aspect to consider with the word *stubborn.* It implies that the dog *absolutely knows* that there is a good reason to do what we want, but still resolutely refuses. He refuses to be persuaded "to do" something else.

And how do we interpret that? Is the dog being bad? Being obstinate? Obsessed? Determined? Perhaps.

What's really going on?

Here we need to comprehend the difference between dogs' brains and our brains. People obviously have the capacity to refuse to respond to another person's request or persuasion. It can be accepted that their minds are thinking: "I refuse to do what you want", or rather "I don't care, and I'm not listening to your point of view".

Dogs really don't think like that.

Dogs simply apply a value to an object or situation and then consider which is best. In the dog's mind, the ball behind the door is worth a million pounds. Just imagine where our focus would be if we considered that all we had to do was open the door to get to a suitcase full of money? Would we listen to a friend offering a cup of tea and cake? My bet is that we'd be thinking: "Yeah, catch ya later for that!"

Now let's consider that our friend actually had the key to the suitcase that would be freely given once we'd spent some quality time with them, listening to their weekend plans. Where would our focus be?

I guess we're really not that much different to our furry friends. It's just that we are better at solving the puzzle because we understand the consequences.

Put simply, when our dogs are being *stubborn* they simply haven't had the chance to figure out in their minds that coming over and sitting by you is the best way to get the door open.

What's the problem?

The trouble is that, once again, using the word *stubborn* closes our own minds to other possibilities. We subconsciously accept that there is no way to change our dog's mind. No matter what we do, nothing will change.

Guess what... we're right!

But only in that moment.

In that moment, the brain has set itself down one path. It's so acutely focused on its goal that there is no rational brain left in there for us to communicate with.

So what can we do about our stubborn dogs?

There are many reasons why dogs may appear to be *stubborn*. There are a couple of examples below. However, in each situation, it helps to take a step back and consider what the dog is actually thinking and how they are feeling.

1. A dog who paws incessantly at a door to get to a favourite ball: For this wee dog, the ball on the other side of the door is worth that million pounds. When he is so engrossed in his task, there is simply nothing that we can do to stop him. The dog is so intent on the job in hand, he has no brainpower left to hear us. This is where many trainers suggest that folks "go back to basics". First, we need to teach them that it is rewarding to come to us, or to go and lie down, without any distractions (and certainly without said ball around). Gradually the distractions are increased starting with, for example, a low-value toy and progressing step–by-step towards the favourite ball (or whatever the dog is obsessing about). It's also possible that this dog is a bit bored and introducing general training and more play with you will probably help.

2. A dog who refuses to move on a walk: In this situation there is, most often, something worrying the dog. Usually, something has happened. Perhaps they had a fright in the past caused by a car backfiring, or perhaps they're scared of a dog or person just along the road. Or, puppies on their first few ventures beyond the garden are often simply overwhelmed with the outside world and need time to adjust. True it is possible that there's something valuable in the opposite direction, but most of the time this is fear. Some calm, reward-based heel training will probably help, as may an exciting and distracting toy.

Summary

So please stop being stubborn about thinking *stubborn.* Try to get inside your dog's head and look for reasons behind their determined behaviour. We will then be able to give ourselves options for taking a different course of action with our dogs.

Of course, this can sometimes be quite difficult and may need a more holistic approach. That's where a qualified and experienced behaviourist or trainer will be able to help you - don't struggle on alone.

He's Stupid!

We think: *He just won't learn anything.*

Dogz Think: *How can I listen to you when therez so many exciting thingz going on!*

What are we talking about?

Some owners decide that their dog is not very bright because he appears not to understand basic commands (or cues). Certain breeds of dogs are often assumed to be more or less intelligent than others because of the speed with which humans have been able to teach them.

What's really going on?

From Border Collies to Bulldogs the *intelligence* level of dogs hardly varies. What makes one dog appear to be a faster learner than another is down to their motivation to perform certain tasks and their willingness to please humans.

Over centuries dogs have been selectively bred for certain purposes - collies love to herd things, bull breeds love to tug things, terriers love to hunt things and so on. Humans have selected these traits repeatedly over many dog generations. In other words, they are born with a desire to perform these tasks. We call these instinctive, inherited behaviours "intrinsic motor patterns".

The dogs we live with today will have inherited a set of intrinsic motor patterns from their parents and these will form the basis of what makes our dog tick. So, the motivation to perform certain tasks will be strongly affected by what we are offering in return.

In addition to this, some breeds have had what we call "biddability" bred into them - these tend to be the breeds designed to work collaboratively with humans (think collies and gun dogs). If a breed was designed to work independently, they will be far less biddable (think terriers, hounds and bull breeds). When you ask a biddable dog to jump, they'll say "how high?". Ask a less biddable breed the same thing and they'll say "why?".

However, no matter what the breed or instincts, training so often goes wrong because we set the dogs up to fail by trying to work with them in environments that are simply too distracting. Consider trying to learn Japanese in the middle of a busy fairground!

What's the problem?

If we label our dogs *stupid* then we stop trying to connect with them, we stop bothering to find out what makes them tick and we seriously limit our opportunities to get the most out of our relationship with them. Dogs are not *stupid*; they just speak a different language to us. If we speak to them in their language, we'll get the response we've been looking for.

So, what can we do about our stupid dogs?

There are a few different aspects to consider:

1. It's quite likely that it may take more time to train the less "biddable" breed, but this is not always the case. It's also about individuality. There are Border Collies who prefer their independence and there are Jack Russells with superb human communication skills.

2. We need to learn to work with our dog's natural desire and not against it. We need to find out what they perceive as rewarding and offer that as payment when training. If your dog is not motivated by food, expecting him to work for food is pointless. But a game of tug or a ball to chase might be just what he'd love! If you have one of the less biddable breeds you'll need to work harder to show them why they should bother.

3. We can, however, help our dogs to learn that there can be different types of reward in life. A toy-focused dog can learn to work for treats, and a food-focused dog can learn to work for a toy. Dogs who don't like being stroked can learn to love your attention. We simply need to take the time to help them to broaden their perspective on the good things in life.

4. Finally, however, the most common problem is that we try to train our dogs when they are too distracted by the environment or other dogs or people. When a dog becomes highly excited or if they feel anxious, they simply can't actually focus on you. Training needs to start with no distraction, and then progress through various levels of difficulty.

For instance:

Example One

Laddie is a one-year-old male Jack Russell Terrier. His owner has tried unsuccessfully to get him to come back on walks around their local fields. He won't even come to her for the tastiest of food treats and prefers to race off into the undergrowth leaving her standing abandoned on the footpath until he deigns to return. She thinks he is too *stupid* to understand that she has liver cake.

Laddie knows full well that his owner has liver cake but liver cake is no substitute for chasing rodents on the edge of the fields! So - Laddie's owner got him a Chase'n'tug toy (www.trixiespetbehaviourandtraining.com/new-products/) and used it regularly at home until Laddie really loved it. Now she takes the Chase'n'tug on walks and regularly plays games with Laddie during the walk. She is now rewarding Laddie for coming away from the activity he loves, by offering a similarly high-value activity.

Example Two

Clover is a two-year-old female English Bull Terrier. Her owner is fed up of Clover head-butting people when she greets them. Clover has injured many visitors and despite many attempts to push her off and teach her to keep her feet on the floor to greet people, she continues to do it. Clover's owner thinks she is just too *stupid* to understand that head-butting humans is not a good thing!

However, by looking at how Clover *feels* and considering her underlying motivation, *her* owner now understands that Clover actually loves rough contact with humans, and that being pushed off is actually rewarding for her. He has worked on lots of carefully controlled tug games with Clover - tugging only continues if feet stay on the floor. He has taught Clover to fetch a tug toy when visitors arrive so now she has a rewarding activity to do instead of jumping up.

He's Just a Bit Timid...

We think: *He's just shy because he's been in the rescue centre for a while.*

Dogz Think: *My world has closed down and I really can't cope with new thingz.*

What are we talking about?

Fortunately, many rescue dogs adjust and resettle into new homes and surroundings quite well. Sadly though, some appear to become aggressive, barky, jumpy, clingy or overly needy for instance.

Some people think that these dogs are just a bit timid or shy or a little fearful. They think that by coaxing them and showing them that humans are kind, they will come out of their shells, realise they've been "rescued" and begin to relax and enjoy the company of dogs and people.

In addition, there are some puppies who seem to want to hide away from people or other puppies in the class, even going so far as to tuck themselves away under a chair.

What's really going on?

Fear is the most important emotion for survival. Our brains prioritise fear over every other emotion because treating things as potentially dangerous will keep us alive. Dog and human brains work in exactly the same way in this respect. Fear memories are stored in the primitive, reactive part of the brain called the amygdala. The amygdala stores the sights, sounds and smells of every frightening event it encounters. It then triggers a fearful reaction to anything that seems *vaguely similar* to any of the fearful events that are stored in the memory banks. The dog has no control over this instinctive, reactive reflex response. For puppies, these fearful memories appear to be inherited to some degree, and it's quite common for an anxious mother or father to produce fearful puppies.

In addition, as already discussed, early, careful socialisation is a very important part of puppy development. If that is lacking or goes wrong in any way, we may end up with a timid puppy or adult.

What's the problem?

If we coax or lure a frightened or nervous dog, we are dragging them out of their "comfort zone" and potentially pushing them into panic. This causes a dangerous situation in which the dog may feel obliged to come towards something it is fearful of, only to then feel overwhelmed by panic and forced to resort to "fight or flight".

So what can we do about our timid dogs?

In general, we need to give the dog or puppy time, and allow the dog to choose what he wants to do or where he wants to be. Don't coax, but allow the dog plenty of opportunity to investigate "scary" things or people at a distance they feel comfortable with. Reward the dog for brave choices and allow the dog to retreat as often and as far as they need.

However, helping a timid dog can be far more complex than we would expect. Most of us probably tend to focus on some obvious behaviour such as barking at visitors or pulling on the lead or lunging at dogs. We focus directly on the behaviour that troubles "us" most. We focus on the things that annoy "us" and that "we" have difficulty with. These are the things that we want fixed.

For the dog, however, there are usually many other issues. For instance, he may be scared of noise, he may feel a little unsettled when left at home alone or he may be experiencing pain. It's very difficult for us to feel comfortable when we are scared (think about a person with arachnophobia sitting in a room with a couple of spiders). We may have difficulty concentrating when we have toothache. Again, the same is true for our dogs.

Therefore on many occasions, it helps to take a step back and consider the full range of issues that a timid dog has to cope with. We can then start to build a more holistic approach to help him.

Example One

A rescue dog is taken to the park and released off lead into a gang of 10 other dogs to "get him used to other dogs". He feels terrified and overwhelmed. Instead of "getting used to it", all his worst fears about other dogs and not trusting humans are confirmed and he fights his way out of there!

Example Two

A rescue dog is taken on lead to an area the other side of the dog park fence and allowed to just hang out watching the other dogs and getting rewarded for doing normal stuff like sniffing while other dogs are within sight. He is never worried that the other dogs will "mug" him and has plenty of time to observe them from a safe distance. He eventually learns to trust his human to keep him safe and that other dogs are not so bad.

He's Guilty

We think: *My dog knows he's done wrong – that's why he looks so guilty.*

Dogz Think: *I don't understand – you are scaring me!*

What are we talking about?

We come home and find our dog has urinated in the house, destroyed a pair of trainers, an item of clothing or chewed the furniture – all things we have consistently told him off for. He may come rushing to greet us, but then looks guilty and slinks off.

What's really going on?

Here's an example. You come home and your dog is running up to you excitedly, happy to say hello. Then you see your chewed up trainers and say "what have you done?". Perhaps you pick the trainers up and speak sternly to him. The next day your dog chews another pair of trainers. This time you speak more sternly and perhaps ignore him for a while. The next time you raise your voice. Each time this happens and the more you tell him off, the guiltier he "looks". Eventually your dog stops greeting you and stays away looking "guilty".

What's really happening is that your dog is reacting to how you are behaving. He is confused. He is not linking your behaviour to what he did to the trainers.

He may have chewed the trainers because it gave him some comfort when he was left alone. He may simply enjoy chewing trainers to give him something to do while you are away. While he is chewing he is definitely not thinking that he's being bad and is going to be in trouble.

Over time, when he hears your key in the door he may start to associate it with you behaving strangely. This may make him feel anxious or unsettled. He may lick his lips, look away or slink away from you. He may try to appease you by lowering his head and coming towards you slowly, wagging his tail while it is held low.

So, he may *look* "guilty", but will more likely be *feeling* unsettled, confused, scared or anxious.

What's the problem?

"Guilt" and "shame" are complex human emotions that require us to understand right from wrong. To feel guilt we need to care about how people judge us AFTER we have done something.

Dogs don't have this level of cognitive skill. They simply do what it takes to make them "feel" good. They don't relate your reaction with what they did a while ago.

Dogs really want to just lead a simple, happy and consistent life. If we persist with telling them off then they may start to distrust us. Sometimes we are nice and sometimes we are not.

We cause confusion and conflict in their minds and we risk damaging our relationship with them, potentially impacting further on how they feel about life in general.

So, what can we do about our guilty dogs?

First we need to consider the specific situations and then determine why our dogs are doing what we don't want them to do. Once we ask those questions we may change how we feel about their behaviour. Then we can begin to work out what we need to do to help them feel good/happy/content. This will involve, managing them better, helping them to feel more relaxed and teaching them what we actually want.

Example 1: Chewing the wrong things:

Chewing is comforting and the dog that destroys trainers may simply be trying to cope with being left alone during the day, or perhaps just having some fun. So, change what you do: tidy up your shoes and perhaps leave an old blanket with your scent on for him to use as a comfort blanket.

Of course, he may simply be bored. Increasing his day-to-day activities and leaving him with safe foody-chew toys may help.

Also teach him to settle whilst he's at home alone and teach him not to play with certain items by offering him alternative items and rewarding him for leaving "off limit" items alone.

Many dogs don't actually like being left at home alone. Most learn to cope, but those that don't, may be acting from anxiety or boredom.

Example 2: Dogs that toilet in the home:

Dogs don't feel guilty if they have a toileting accident in the house – they feel relieved! Most dogs naturally toilet outdoors. They may have an "accident" indoors if: they have not been properly house trained; have an infection; are anxious; or simply cannot hold on any more.

We may need to revert to puppy-style house training and/or get them checked by the vet.

ALWAYS set your dog up for success and avoid confusion. Do not put them in situations where they will do what dogs naturally do - and then punish them.

Punishment

We think: I need to tell him off so that he does not do that again.

Dogz Think: What? Me confuzed!

What are we talking about?

Many of us instinctively feel that we should punish our dog when he ignores or disobeys us, growls, bites, pulls on the lead, barks or jumps. We think this will teach him that it's "bad" and that he will learn not to do it again.

For example: We may tell him off for not coming back to us when called; shout at him for jumping on the kitchen worktop; shout and jerk his lead when he pulls; or grab and pull him off the sofa. In dog training, this is called "Positive Punishment". At other times, we may use "Negative Punishment", where we take away something the dog wants such as attention, play or treats.

What's really going on?

Well, it may seem strange that he *knows* how to walk to heel but still pulls sometimes or that he comes to you in the training class but not in the park.

However, he's not being bad. As discussed in the Guilty chapter, dogs simply do whatever they think will make them feel good right now; behaviours associated with good feelings are more likely to be repeated.

Most often, dogs just haven't had enough practise and have additionally had too much opportunity to repeat the unwanted behaviours.

What's the problem?

First we have to ask – does he actually know how I expect him to behave? Has he actually been taught to sit nicely when people greet him for example? Dogs need to be taught in a variety of locations and situations and crucially, taught in such a way that they are actually able to learn. An excited or distracted or anxious dog can't learn effectively.

Punished behaviours become associated with feelings of anxiety, confusion and fear. The danger is that we don't actually know what he will be thinking of when he is being punished. Punishment does sometimes appear to work but the associated undesirable emotions may well create additional problems.

Example 1: When dogs are having fun off lead, they can be so engrossed in what they are doing that they literally cannot pay us attention. When they have eventually had their fill of scents and play they come back to us – only to be told off. They do not link the punishment to the fact that they have ignored us for the last 10 or 20 minutes. Instead, they feel punished for coming back to us. As a consequence they may take longer and longer to come back.

Example 2: Dogs sometimes like to lie on the sofa because it is warm and comfortable. He does not understand why we suddenly appear annoyed or angry when he's not in his own bed. He may be confused, anxious or even angry as he really feels that the sofa is the right place to be. If we then confront him and shout at him or pull him off the furniture, he may growl or snap or even bite. This confrontation serves to escalate the emotional tension.

Overall, if we use punishment to train our dog:

- We become inconsistent and unpredictable – sometimes we're nice and sometimes we're nasty.

- He isn't learning what we actually want him to do.

- He may learn that growling does not work – but biting does.

Example 3: What about punishing a dog from a distance with, say, a punishment collar? If you are not there he cannot associate that with you right? It is possible that the jolt may interrupt him and he'll come running back to you or dart off the sofa. However, as dogs relate their present feelings to their immediate situation, he may associate the pain with passing children or dogs (and become fearful or reactive towards children or dogs) or become scared of the sofa or people entering the room. He may even start to guard the whole room or become generally anxious in his home.

The topic of punishment is hotly debated in the dog-training world. "Negative Punishment" is perhaps more acceptable. For example, ignoring a dog when they jump can frequently work. But, many times this actually increases frustration and causes the dog to jump more. Therefore, a careful approach is required.

So, what can we do instead of punishing our dogs?

Successful training frequently requires the combination of management and teaching: preventing bad habits forming whilst teaching and rewarding wanted behaviours. Once he has learned an acceptable successful behaviour, he is unlikely to resort to an unacceptable one.

For instance: If you do not want him on the furniture then consider keeping him out of the room when you're not there. (There is no written rule that dogs are not allowed on furniture.) Separately, work on teaching him to go to a nice comfy bed that you've provided for him in that room. And then, every time he tries to get onto furniture, ask him to go to his bed and reward him for doing so. Or, if he is allowed on furniture, teach him an "on" or an "off" cue, so that he gets on or off when asked.

Further, we can benefit from thinking more broadly about why our dogs "mis-behave". Providing them with enough stimulation and training will prevent boredom and increase patience. Of course, sometimes dogs struggle with fears and other issues in life that impact on our training efforts. If that's the case then please don't struggle on alone but seek help from a good behaviourist or trainer.

Summary

We've seen in this book how labels like *stubborn* or *stupid* may help us get rid of some of our frustration with a wayward dog, but can really stop us understanding what's actually going on. Here's a wee summary of what we've covered:

The Phrase	What We Think	What Dogz Think
He's *Dominant*	My dog always jumps on me and pulls me along.	Heyz, I just wanna have cuddles like we used to when I woz a puppy & I wanna get to the park fast to play with my pals.
He *Hates* the Postie or Cats or the Vacuum	My dog hates these things so much because he is barking, growling, lunging at, or chasing them.	Postie: There must be something very wrong wiv thiz guy. He never comez in - he must not be a friend - I better get rid of him! Cats: Yeah, a catz, I lurv to chase them catz! Vacuum: Geez, that noise is scary!
He's Just *Play Biting*	It hurts a bit but it's ok or He's constantly biting me he is a monster!	But this iz how I play with my dog palz.
About *Rewards*	I don't want to bribe my dog or make them fat, they should just do as I ask because they love me. Plus I don't want to carry food with me all the time.	Heyz, I lovez you okay, but why should I do what you want when therez so many interezting thingz out there?
About *Socialisation*	My puppy or dog needs to play with lots of others so they learn to be tolerant of all dogs.	Heyz, I lovez playing with other puppiez, I get so excited! Or weeelll, I like to take my time meeting others n hang back til I'm sure we'll get along. Those big dogz look scary.
He's *Stubborn*	My dog knows what to do, he just won't do what I want.	But it'z a rabbitzzzz!
He's *Stupid*!	He just won't learn anything.	How can I listen to you when therez so many exciting thingz going on!
He's Just a *Bit Timid*...	He's just shy because he's been in the rescue centre for a while.	My world has clozed down and I really can't cope with new thingz.
He's *Guilty*	My dog knows he's done wrong – that's why he looks so guilty.	I don't understand – you are scaring me!
Punishment	I need to tell him off so that he does not do that again.	What? Me confuzed!

www.facebook.com/DogzThinkzDifferentz/
www.pawsability.co.uk/DogzThinkzDifferentz

Printed in Great
Britain
by Amazon